What Makes a Champion?

Written by Patrick Lay

Flying Start
to Literacy®

T0363495

Contents

Introduction

What makes a champion?
What makes a person the best of the best?

Is natural ability the most important factor in becoming
a champion? There are many people with natural ability
who do not become champions. So there must be more
to becoming a champion than just natural ability.

Qualities such as determination, self-motivation,
resilience and having a positive attitude must all be
parts of the puzzle. The desire to practise and perfect
a skill would also help make a champion.

The lives of four different sporting champions show the unique ups and downs each one encountered along the way to becoming a champion.

As you read about these fascinating people and their remarkable lives, you will find out what things contributed to make each of them a champion.

Chapter 1

Bethany Hamilton
Surfing inspiration

The ambulance siren wailed as it made its way to the hospital. Inside, in critical condition, was surfing prodigy, 13-year-old Bethany Hamilton. The unthinkable had happened – a four-metre long tiger shark had attacked her in the water as she surfed. Bethany had lost her arm and was fighting for her life. In that one horrible moment of terror, Bethany's world was turned upside down.

Childhood

Bethany Hamilton was born in 1990 in Hawaii in the United States where she grew up. Her family loved to surf and for as long as Bethany could remember, she had also loved to surf. When she surfed, she had amazing balance in the water, a graceful style and a natural feel for the waves. From the age of eight, she was consistently winning surfing competitions and was hopeful that one day she would become a professional surfer.

Her family were extremely supportive of her ambitious goal. She was home-schooled so that she could spend time practising and travelling to different surfing competitions. It was clear to everyone who knew Bethany that she had all the characteristics of a world-class surfer. Her future as a surfing champion looked certain.

Career in the balance

One morning in 2003, when Bethany was surfing, she was attacked by a shark. Bethany's life was hanging in the balance and her childhood dream of becoming a professional surfer seemed to be over. She lost almost half of the blood from her body and was rushed into emergency surgery in a battle to save her life.

Bethany survived the surgery, but tragically lost her left arm. Her friends, family and community assumed that losing her arm meant the end of Bethany's surfing dream. Bethany initially had the same thought, but only two days after having surgery on her arm, she was planning her return to the water.

Amazingly, 28 days after the shark attack, Bethany re-entered the ocean with her surfboard under her right arm. Could she possibly surf? Would she be brave enough to risk another attack? She didn't know the answers to these questions, but she wanted to find out.

"Strive to find things to be thankful for, and just look for the good in who you are!"
Bethany Hamilton

Bethany is an immensely positive person and her
never-say-die attitude kicked in once she was back doing
the thing she loved most. At first, she couldn't stand up
on her board, but she kept on trying. Eventually, she was
able to push herself up to a standing position with the
use of only one arm. Her incredible balance, brilliant
technique, knowledge of the ocean and determination
allowed her to stay upright as she rode the waves. She
was surfing again!

Moving on

After she went surfing for the first time since her accident, Bethany started to surf regularly again.

She wanted to compete again, but realised that to do it seriously, she would now have to be stronger, fitter and healthier than every other competitor. Bethany started a rigorous training routine of running, lifting weights, exercising and eating nutritious food. She also trained harder and longer in the water to perfect her skills.

Her effort was rewarded. In 2005, Bethany once again felt the thrill of victory when she won her first competition since her debilitating accident. Bethany was back! In 2007, she realised her dream of becoming a professional surfer and went on to win several professional competitions.

Bethany's teen milestones

Age 13: Takes 2nd place at NSSA National Championships

Age 13: Loses left arm in shark attack

Age 14: Releases best-selling autobiography, *Soul Surfer*

Age 15: Wins the US national under-18 surf championships

Age 18: Takes 3rd place at Roxy Pro Gold Coast, Australia

Out of the water, Bethany's life also blossomed. She became a motivational speaker and a positive role model to people throughout the world. She is now married and has a son, Tobias.

So, what made Bethany Hamilton a champion? Bethany showed us that a champion uses natural ability, determination and bravery to overcome the hurdles they confront. In Bethany's case, the hurdle seemed insurmountable, but her faith, persistence and hard work allowed her to reach her dream and more.

Chapter 2

Pelé
Soccer
sensation

"Pelé! Pelé! Pelé!" Imagine a 100,000-strong crowd chanting your name as you dribble the ball down the field, playing for your country in the final of the World Cup. For Brazil's Pelé, this scene was a reality. Known for his brilliant attacking style and natural flair, Pelé didn't disappoint his fans in the final of the 1970 World Cup when he headed the first goal of the match. His team went on to win the World Cup and, for Pelé, it was the beginning of his journey to become a legend of the game, and one of the best players ever!

Childhood

Edson Arantes do Nascimento (better known by his nickname, Pelé) was born on 23 October 1940 and grew up in a poor district of São Paulo, Brazil. From humble beginnings, Pelé became, arguably, the greatest soccer player of all time.

Pelé's father was also a talented soccer player. He had a short career, but he scored a lot of goals and he gave Pelé his first soccer lessons. Pele's family struggled to make much money so, as a young boy, Pelé had to earn money for the family by doing different jobs such as shining shoes or waiting tables.

Pelé (centre) with his mum and dad, 1958

13

Playing soccer

From the moment he was old enough to kick a ball,
Pelé loved soccer. He played for hour upon hour in
the streets near his home. Pelé didn't always own a
soccer ball so he sometimes used a large grapefruit or
made a ball from old rags tied up with string.

Pelé had an abundance of natural ability. He was
agile, strong, quick, flexible and extremely coordinated.
Hours of endless practice sharpened his natural
ability and Pelé soon developed his own unique,
almost magical, technique.

Pelé was by far the best soccer player in his local area. In 1956, at the age of 15, he decided to try out for a professional club. Not surprisingly, due to his incredible talent and astonishing speed, he was signed by the Santos Football Club. Pelé moved away from home, and from everything that was safe and familiar to him, to start his professional soccer career.

When he was 15, he played his first game of professional soccer. So stunning were his early games, that only ten months later he was picked to play for Brazil's national team.

"Success is no accident. It is hard work, perseverance learning, studying, sacrifice and most of all, love of what you are doing or learning to do."
Pelé

World Cup career

Pelé's first World Cup was a Cinderella story.
Brazil stunned the world to win the championship
and Pelé became the youngest player ever to be
part of a World Cup winning side – he was 17.
He kicked six goals during the tournament and
his individual highlight was scoring three goals
(a hat-trick) in the semi-final against France.

At the next World Cup, in 1962, Pelé played for Brazil
again. Brazil defended its championship and Pelé scored
some goals, but he was injured and missed playing in
most of the games.

The Brazilian team crashed out in sensational fashion in
the early rounds of the 1966 World Cup in England. Pelé
was devastated and thought about retiring from soccer.
He didn't, and in 1970, he played for Brazil in another
World Cup final. Pelé's role as an accurate and powerful
striker with the ability to use both sides of his body
enabled his team to be extremely successful. With Pelé as
a star player, the Brazilian team once again excited the
football world by winning the championship for a record
third time. Pelé became a legend.

"I was born to play football, just like Beethoven was born to write music and Michelangelo was born to paint."
Pelé

During his football career, Pelé led his team to six championships for Brazil. He scored 1281 career goals as a professional player and was named Player of the Century. He retired from playing soccer in 1974.

So, what made Pelé a champion? He had great natural ability, but he was also immensely passionate about soccer. These two things combined to make him one of the most successful athletes of all time.

Pelé's trophy cabinet

Won three FIFA World Cups:
1958 Sweden
1962 Chile
1970 Mexico

Chapter 3

Evonne Goolagong Cawley

Trailblazing tennis player

Did you know there was a time when a sportsperson was banned from some sporting competitions because of the colour of their skin? Thankfully, this prejudice doesn't exist in modern sport.

One person who helped to break down racial barriers was a young Aboriginal called Evonne Goolagong. Evonne, a star in her own right, became a trailblazer for many others. She has been the number one tennis player in the world and her impressive career has paved the way for future indigenous Australian sportspeople.

Childhood

Evonne was born in 1951 and grew up in a small country town in New South Wales. She was one of eight children and her parents were from the Wiradjuri nation.

Evonne had a happy childhood. She did, however, grow up with the fear of being taken away from her parents. At that time in Australia, many young Aboriginal children were taken from their families to live in the "white world". Luckily, this did not happen to Evonne.

Evonne always loved tennis. Her life changed forever when her talent was recognised by tennis coach Vic Edwards. He encouraged Evonne's parents to allow her to move to Sydney when she was 13 so that he could coach her.

The move to Sydney was not always easy for the shy 13-year-old. She faced prejudice and racism as she was the only Aboriginal kid in a mainly "white world". Despite these hardships and missing her family, Evonne was determined to keep improving her tennis. And that she did!

Career

Evonne was an outstanding junior player. She won tournaments in every age group as she progressed through the junior ranks. Her mix of skill and power, along with her flowing natural movement, made her almost unstoppable.

In 1970, at the age of 19, Evonne left Australia to play in tournaments all around the world. She won an impressive seven out of 21 tournaments in her first year. The next year, in 1971, she turned professional and incredibly she won two grand slam singles events – the French Open and Wimbledon. She had achieved her childhood dream of not only playing at Wimbledon, but also winning it! She won the famous tournament a second time in 1980.

Although Evonne was known throughout the world, she still experienced discrimination. Even after she had won her first Wimbledon championship, she was once refused entry into a music venue, simply because she was an Aboriginal.

Evonne Goolagong Cawley
wins Wimbledon, 1 July 1971

Evonne retired in 1983 after winning eight grand slam titles and 92 tournaments in total. Her amazing career came at a time when it was common for Aboriginal people to be treated unfairly. This makes her achievements all the more outstanding.

"Mum's words always stay in my mind. She used to tell me to 'have a lovely day' whenever I left the house to go play. When I came home she always asked, 'Did you have a lovely day?' It was never, 'Did you win or lose?'"

21

Legacy

As the first-ever indigenous Australian to play tennis on the professional tour, Evonne has left a lasting legacy. She is an inspirational role model to many, particularly young Aboriginal people. Since her retirement, Evonne has combined her pride in her indigenous heritage and her love of tennis, to help others. She has done this in a variety of ways – working on committees, running tennis clinics and working for charities.

From 1998 to 2005, Evonne was a "Tennis Ambassador" for Tennis Australia. Her main role was to increase the number of women playing tennis throughout Australia.

In 2012, Evonne established the Evonne Goolagong Foundation to help young indigenous people to "Dream-Believe-Learn-Achieve". The Foundation runs programs that encourage young Aboriginal people to stay at school while they follow their dreams to become sports professionals.

So, what makes a champion? Evonne showed us that sometimes having enormous talent isn't enough. Evonne also needed bravery, determination and perseverance to breakdown racial barriers and overcome unfair discrimination to become a champion.

Evonne's Hall of Fame

TENNIS COURT

1985: Sport Australia Hall
of Fame

1988: International Tennis Hall
of Fame

1989: Aboriginal and Islander
Sports Hall of Fame

1989: International Women's
Sports Hall of Fame

Chapter 4

Dylan
Alcott
All-around champion

Loving life and inspiring others to be the best they can be! Standing on a podium, holding a gold medal, singing your country's national anthem... this is a scene that many athletes only get to dream of. For Dylan Alcott, this was a reality when he was just 17 years old.

In 2008, he was a member of the gold-medal winning Australian Paralympic basketball team. For Dylan, this gold medal was only the beginning.

Childhood

Dylan was born with a tumour wrapped around his spinal cord. He underwent a long and difficult operation to have it removed. The operation saved his life, but Dylan became a paraplegic. He couldn't walk and has used a wheelchair ever since.

In his early teens, Dylan struggled with how he felt about his disability. His strength of character and optimistic outlook allowed him to work through his feelings and he developed a positive view on life. Dylan realised that he could achieve anything that he wanted to. And that is what he did. Dylan Alcott has led an incredibly inspiring and successful life.

Career

At age 15, Dylan decided to take his sporting career seriously. He aimed to be picked for the Australian Paralympic basketball team, the *Rollers*. He trained hard and was selected. The *Rollers* won gold at the 2008 Paralympics, making Dylan the youngest ever wheelchair basketball gold medallist.

Dylan represented Australia with the *Rollers* again in 2010 at the World Championships where his dynamic play saw him named in the World All-Star team. In 2012, as a member of the *Rollers*, Dylan and the team came away with a silver medal at the London Paralympics.

"To reach the pinnacle of two Paralympic sports and win gold in both sports ... if you told me that when I was a little kid ... I would've said, 'No way, mate!'"

Dylan Alcott

The challenge of representing his country in one sport wasn't enough for Dylan. In 2013, he decided to put all of his efforts into his other great sporting love – tennis. Since his change of focus, Dylan has played in tournaments all around the world and has achieved great success. The highlights of his tennis career were winning the 2015 Australian, French and US Opens respectively. He finished 2015 ranked as the world number one wheelchair tennis player.

But Dylan's next burning sporting goal was still to come. At the 2016 Rio Paralympics, he won both the men's singles and doubles tennis competition! This incredible athlete now has gold medals in two Paralympic sports – basketball and tennis.

27

Giving back

Dylan is a captivating and natural motivational speaker. His message is simple and yet powerful – a person with a disability can do anything that an able-bodied person can do.

One of Dylan's aims is to raise awareness and change the community's perceptions of disability. His talks are full of positive messages, delivered with charm and humour. Dylan embraces his disability and vows that he wouldn't want his life to be any other way.

Dylan also works hard to "give back" to the many charities that helped him when he was young. Dylan organised a fundraising event at which he aimed to play tennis for 24 hours. With typical Dylan Alcott determination, he achieved this goal and, along the way, raised $110,000 for children's charities. What a champion!

Dylan's Paralympic medal tally

2008: Gold, Beijing
Wheelchair Basketball

2012: Silver, London
Wheelchair Basketball

2016: Gold, Rio
Tennis Men's Quad Singles

2016: Gold, Rio
Tennis Men's Quad Doubles

Dylan's long-term ambition is to work in the media, either on television or in the press, to spread his message. He believes that this would go a long way to help normalise disability.

So, what makes a champion? In Dylan's case it is a mixture of physical and psychological strength, natural skills and a "never-say-die" attitude. Dylan epitomises the "glass half-full" approach to life.

Conclusion

There are many aspects to being a sporting champion. The common thread among so many who excel in their chosen sport is their determination to be the best they can be, and their ability to overcome obstacles that are placed in their way. Sheer hard work and tenacity, mixed with natural athleticism and skill, go a long way to enabling athletes to achieve their goals.

Many sporting champions, by their example, teach us lessons about how to succeed at sport. And, just as importantly, these champions also teach us lessons in how to live our lives!

"I guess I just like to challenge myself and push myself harder to do things that I don't think I can, to do things that other people do not think I can. It pushes me. I push my own personal limits."

Bethany Hamilton

"Success isn't determined by how many times you win, but by how you play the week after you lose."

Pelé

"I believe that's what life is all about (having fun). I certainly had a lot of fun during my career playing tennis, doing the thing I wanted to do and to do it well."

Evonne Goolagong Cawley

"One of the most important things in life is to have a purpose and to have a passion... I'm just a testament to somebody that has become the best version of themselves and I've used the most out of my situation and got the most out of my life."

Dylan Alcott

Bethany, Pelé, Evonne and Dylan are just some of the people that we can by inspired by. Bethany persevered when other people may have given up altogether. Pelé was so enthusiastic about his career that nothing was going to stand in his way. Evonne was ambitious and determined to succeed. Dylan was so incredibly motivated that he did not see any limitations to his goals.

There are many, many other people who play sport and do the best they can who may never come to the public's attention, but who are still champions because they give it everything they've got.